CLOUD COMPUTING

A Comprehensive Guide to Cloud Computing

Austin Young

TABLE OF CONTENTS

Introduction...3

Chapter 1...6

Before Cloud Computing.............................6

Misunderstandings about Cloud

Computing..9

How Cloud Computing Works.....................17

Chapter 2...19

Types of Cloud Computing..........................19

Chapter 3...70

Cloud deployment models...........................70

Chapter 4..142

Virtualization and Cloud Computing.........142

Chapter 5..153

Cloud Computing vs Grid Computing........153

Chapter 6..156

Cloud Computing Adoption........................156

Chapter 7..161

Conclusion...161

Other Books by Same Author......................163

Introduction

Cloud computing has to do with any form of hosted service provided through the internet. These services sometimes consist of storage, analytics, networks, software, databases, servers, and other computing operations implemented over the cloud. The word "Cloud" comes from a network design utilized by network engineers to exemplify the positioning of several network devices and their interconnection. The structure of this network design looked like a cloud. Users on the service can access programs and files kept in the cloud whenever, eradicating the necessity to continually be close to a physical hardware. External parties host programs and information, which are stored on a universal network of protected datacenters rather than on the user's storage drive. This enables protected mobile access, expedites collaboration and sharing, and frees up processing power irrespective of the user's location or device type. Cloud computing is a more proficient method of distributing computing resources. With this, service and software resources are subscription-based, meaning that consumers pay a monthly fee as opposed to procuring licenses. Providers manage the platforms and software, while constantly providing updates for maximum security and performance. Users can increase their capacity to accommodate business growth since computing power is isolated rather than centralized. Numerous people can retrieve a shared file or program and work together concurrently from varying locations.

For instance, previously, spreadsheets and documents created by users were stored in a disk, USB drive or physical hard drive. The saved files were unreachable outside the computer they were created on, if there were no forms of external hardware component, emails or some other forms of services for saving and transferring data. The emergence of the cloud has led to fewer people worrying about corrupted or lost USB drives, or fried hard drives. With cloud computing, these documents are accessible all over since the data exists on interconnected hosted servers that convey data through the internet. In addition to that, previously, a company needing to set up an IT infrastructure would typically install the networking resources, software and servers it requires. However, with cloud computing, almost every one of those resources and services are available through third parties that provide such in the cloud. The company will not have to invest a lot of money in hardware nor spend so much time managing that hardware. Rather, they can set up precisely the correct size and type of computing resources required to operate their IT department. Resources can be accessed almost immediately, while paying for only what is used.

Chapter 1

Before Cloud Computing

Conventional business applications are costly and problematic. The assortment and amount of software and hardware needed to operate them were overwhelming. Companies required an entire team of specialists to operate, protect, modify, set up, analyze, install, and configure them. When this effort is multiplied across numerous applications, it becomes clear to see why it was difficult for small and midsize companies to get customized solutions. This was only possible for larger companies with great IT departments. Improvements in cloud computing have transformed that. Cloud computing has eradicated or restructured many of the features associated with setting up traditional IT infrastructure:

- Earlier, employees had to email documents back and forth; where at a time, there would be multiple versions of a document saved locally on numerous devices as well as occurrences of employees making changes to their version of the document. Files stored in the cloud with shared permissions are always current, there can be assurance that all employees are working on the same file with similar information.

- There was always the fear that a natural disaster or an emergency could destroy all the records of a company, since information saved physically in the company's computers is susceptible to failure or loss. Information saved in the cloud has several more protections.
- Updates to software used to entail huge expenses after some years, in order to acquire the most recent version of essential programs. There

was manual application installation and maintenance on every device. Only the major organizations could employ software developers to develop custom-made software. Security issues and defects might not be resolved for a long time.

- A specific geographic work location can no longer hinder an employee's access to information and processes; with the cloud, they can work remotely and still be as productive.

- Physically backing up data on discs, hard drives, or other devices is no longer necessary.

- Even though technology professionals are still sought after by companies, there is no longer a need for specialized experts to troubleshoot software and hardware systems, as monotonous activities like installing updates on computers one after another have been removed.

- Companies no longer have to store groups of servers in equipment rooms or airy closets.

Misunderstandings about Cloud Computing

Some companies might be hesitant about the shift from legacy, in-house systems or applications to an entirely cloud-based infrastructure. Several concerns regarding the cloud are due to common, sometimes outdated misconceptions. Some of these are noted below:

- **Cloud systems are not secure**
  Some technical and operational executives are worried that the cloud is not safe or at a minimum not as safe as the in-house systems. The significance for security in businesses today cannot

be overstated, so these executives have the right to be vigilant. Bearing in mind the delicate nature of client data that companies save, particularly financial or personal information, it is rational that technology experts want to have thorough assurance in the infrastructures they depend on. With that understood, it is important to note that while in-house infrastructures maintain data within the company's firewall, it does not denote that it is resistant to threats. A good example of this would be the Equifax breach in 2017.

In many instances, the cloud is safer than in-house systems because of the cloud provider's commitment to and focus on continuous security procedures. Not only do cloud providers have assigned in-house resources, they also frequently depend on external inspections to preserve certifications and compliance, and help clients in validating security processes and policies. They utilize several industry standards like Federal Risk and Authorization Management Program (FedRAMP), Service Organization Controls 2 (SOC2), Health Insurance Portability & Accountability Act (HIPAA), General Data Protection Regulation (GDPR), or Payment Card Industry (PCI). The cloud provider's operation is reliant on security, uptime and dependability. For example, big cloud-based facilities such as Office 365 and G Suite are reinforced by systems that regularly installs patches and updates, which aids regulate security threats. This liberates the company from the burden of handling the entire security of the systems and installing updates.

However, companies should know that there is no business that is wholly protected from security breaches irrespective of their system architecture. Security is typically still the company's obligation after moving across the physical layer. There is the requirement to make certain that the data is encrypted at all times, security groups and network ACLs are organized, and servers' operating systems are safe. Cloud computing makes this easier to accomplish, since the tools to complete a number of these fundamental tasks are sometimes already included, or easily accessible as an add-on to other services — that would have been more expensive or more problematic otherwise. Businesses that make intelligent decisions regarding their architecture, may transfer the responsibility of several modules to a cloud provider through the utilization of regulated services. One good example for the occasion where the management of the operating system is no longer the company's is RDS for databases.

- **Absence of appropriate encryption in the cloud**
  Many people get the wrong idea about the implementation of encryption to maintain data securely. For instance, encryption is mostly utilized for data-in-transit, where data is safeguarded against been seen from anyone as it moves from a particular internet address to a different one. However, data-at-rest can also be encrypted,

where data stored in a system is encrypted. Considering this, a company have to know the form of encryption it needs. When it is time to select the suitable cloud service, it would be good to know about the security processes that a cloud architecture executes and determine how it can guard the company's data.

- **Intermingling of client data in multi-tenant cloud systems**
When a company seeks some services of a cloud provider, they turn out to be one of numerous clients, with all existing on the same cloud infrastructure. This led to a worry that data is getting mixed up, that data in one company is visible to other companies on the same infrastructure, and that on the premise that a single account is hacked it's simple to gain

entrance to a different company's sensitive client data. This does not apply to cloud-native resources. Cloud providers makes major effort to guarantee that hosted data is only accessible by the company that owns it; thus, their software infrastructures are purposely developed to certify that. Additionally, inserting new customers to the infrastructure is really an advantage to existing tenants. Since it is easier for the cloud provider to comprehend network activities and augment performance preemptively when there is more data to work with.

- **Companies are no more accountable for data security when on the cloud**
  Even though cloud security is vital, safeguarding data eventually depends on the consumers with access. Losing

unlocked business mobile phones or computers can leave data exposed and undermine the company's whole cloud architecture. That is why it is suggested to always have robust verification techniques ready for devices used to gain entrance to the cloud.

- **The cloud is never out of order**
Similar to other technological resources, cloud-based resources are not resistant to technical problems. For instance, some cloud providers have experienced server failures and outages that damaged files and possibly data loss in the process. An additional cause of failure for cloud services is hacking. Utilizing a cloud service that is not optimal and is susceptible to attacks can result in deleted or stolen data, which can be

difficult to recover if there are no offline backups. It is necessary to clarify with a cloud provider about the guaranteed features, before committing to any form of cloud service. Several cloud providers make assurances concerning a service's safety or its uptime for provider-connected breaches.

How Cloud Computing Works

Cloud computing consist of two features backend and frontend. Frontend is the user-facing aspect of the cloud involving user interactions. It encompasses applications and interfaces that are essential to gain entrance to the cloud infrastructure. Whereas backend includes the software and hardware that are needed for cloud computing operations. This consists of security mechanisms, data storage, servers, virtual machines, etc. The cloud provider manages it. The backend is responsible for managing data security, traffic control and regulating protocols. Each application in the cloud has a host, the cloud provider is tasked with sustaining the huge datacenters that offer the computing power, storage capacity, and security required to retain every information sent by the users to the cloud. Cloud providers can sell the privileges to utilize their clouds as well as save data on their systems, while also presenting to the customer an environment for interconnection between programs and devices.

Chapter 2

Types of Cloud Computing

There are three types of cloud computing, commonly referred to as Software-as-a-Service (SaaS), Platform-as-a-Service (PaaS), and Infrastructure-as-a-Service (IaaS). Choosing the appropriate type of cloud computing needed, can assist in striking the right amount of control and avoid undifferentiated heavy lifting.

- **Software-as-a-Service (SaaS)**
  This refers to a method for distributing software, wherein a service provider or vendor hosts applications which are made available to clients over the internet. Through multitenant architecture, SaaS strictly offers business software to tons of customers. All the elements that describe a software, from algorithms, codes, and scripts, along with the physical

hardware (in terms of the structures and servers that store them) are retained and maintained by the providers in their own facilities. SaaS is turning out to be an increasingly predominant delivery model and an underlying technology that supports Web Services or Service Oriented Architecture (SOA). Via the internet, this solution is available to users everywhere. Previously, software application was required to be purchased upfront, after which it is installed on the computer. On the other hand, SaaS users pay for subscriptions to the software instead of purchasing it. Some SaaS solutions are offered free, but many entail an annual or monthly subscription to retain the service. Requiring no management or hardware installation, SaaS solutions are very successful in the business world. Many important tasks such as planning, invoicing, sales, and accounting can be carried out using SaaS.

SaaS deployment model

This has to do with the way cloud providers use the internet to distribute software and bill their users, who simply run the software on the browsers of their mobile devices or computers—all the software being managed by the provider's servers. This multi-tenant, provider-hosted processing and server model is the opposite of the traditional on-site model of deploying software. The low barrier to implementation of this model has encouraged trial and freemium opportunities through which most users originally experience the product. Because of its web delivery format, SaaS eliminates the requirement to download and install software on each individual computer, which is not a pleasant prospect for any IT staff. Providers manage all of the possible technical issues such as storage, servers, middleware, and data, while companies can simply streamline their support and maintenance.

The deployment model of SaaS is comparable to the establishment stage of a utility amenity, which is followed by billing and metering at regular interims for the amenities that have been provided. A SaaS provider through a user provisioning procedure, which is often automated, typically initiates SaaS deployment. Consecutively, a third-party-managed (hosted) services vendor can initiate

SaaS deployment. SaaS deployment is regarded as complete as soon as a user has the required method to access a SaaS solution, irrespective of whether the user starts using the service after it has been provisioned.

Characteristics of SaaS

Below are some ways to aid in determining when SaaS is being used:

- o Users not responsible for software or hardware updates.
- o Administered from a central location.
- o Easily reached over the internet.
- o Hosted on a virtual server by an external provider.
- o Inclusive, offering maintenance, compliance, and security as part of the fee.

o Scalable, with diverse tiers for large, medium and small businesses.

o The capacity for each user to simply customize applications to accommodate their business processes without having an effect on the common infrastructure. Due to the way SaaS is built, these customizations are distinct to each user or company and are always preserved via upgrades. Meaning that SaaS vendors can make upgrades more frequently, with much lower adoption cost and less customer risk.

o A multitenant architecture, where all applications and users share a particular, common code base and infrastructure that is centrally maintained.

Since customers for SaaS providers are all on similar code base and infrastructure, providers can innovate more rapidly and save the valued development time formerly spent on maintaining various versions of outdated code.

When to utilize SaaS

SaaS is an appropriate option for the following:

o For applications that require both mobile and web access.

o A small company or startup that desires to launch ecommerce rapidly, with limited time or resources for resolving server issues.

o For short-term projects necessitating collaboration.

o Applications with inconsistent demand, such as tax software.

Benefits of using SaaS

The essential benefits of SaaS include:

o Access application data from everywhere. Users can access their stored in the cloud from any mobile device or computer connected to the internet. Moreover, data is not lost when a user's device or computer fails, since the data is saved in the cloud.

o Easily mobilize employees. With SaaS, it is easier for companies to mobilize employees, since users can access SaaS data and applications from any mobile device or computer connected to the internet. There is no concern about developing applications to run on various types of devices and computers because the service vendor has already done this. Additionally, there is no need to bring an expert onboard to handle the security problems inherent in cloud computing. A carefully selected service provider will guarantee the security of users' data, irrespective of the kind of device consuming it.

o Users can work on most SaaS applications through their web browser without having to download and set up any software, although some applications require plugins. This indicates that a company does not need to procure and install any special software for its users.

o Easy scalability. Payment is made for only what is utilized, thus saving money since the SaaS solution automatically scales down and up based on the level of usage. That is particularly important for companies whose operations are cyclical in nature, and also for companies that are growing quickly.

o SaaS makes even advanced enterprise applications, like CRM and ERP, affordable for companies that don't have the resources to purchase, deploy, and manage the necessary software and infrastructure themselves.

o SaaS customers also take advantage of the fact that service vendors can set up

automatic updates in software—
mostly on a monthly or weekly
basis—so companies do not
have to be concerned about
installing patches like security
updates, or purchasing new
releases when they are available.
This can be particularly
appealing to companies with
inadequate IT staff to manage
these tasks.

Disadvantages of SaaS

SaaS comes with some challenges and
risks that companies should be aware
of to capitalize on the advantages of
the delivery model. These are:

o Downtime and performance.
   Since the provider manages and
   controls the SaaS service,
   customers rely on providers to
   maintain performance and

security of the service. Network issues, cyber-attacks or unplanned and planned maintenance may affect the performance of the application in spite of adequate Service Level Agreement (SLA) defenses in place.

o Limited modules. Since SaaS applications sometimes come in a standardized format, the choice of modules may be a compromise against performance, cost, security, or other organizational policies. Besides, due to the security, cost or vendor lock-in fears, it may not be feasible to switch services or vendors to serve new feature requests in the future.

o Lack of control. SaaS services effectively involves turning over controls to the external service vendor. These controls are not restricted to the software – with regard to the appearance, updates or version– but also the governance and data. Consequently, customers may have to redefine their data governance and security models to fit the functionality and features of the SaaS service.

o Customization. SaaS applications offer very little capability for customization. Since there is no one-size-fits-all solution, users may be restricted to specific integrations, performance and functionality as offered by the provider. On the other hand, on-site solutions that come with various software development kits offer a wide range of customization options.

o Data security. There may be a need to transfer large amount of data to the remote datacenters of SaaS applications with the intention of performing necessary software operations. Transferring sensitive business data to public-cloud dependent SaaS solution may compromise compliance and security, in addition to incurring significant cost in transferring large data workloads.

o Lack of integration support: Several companies want deep integrations with on-site services, data and applications. The SaaS provider may offer inadequate support in this matter, forcing companies to use internal resources for managing and designing integrations. The difficulty of integrations can further restrict how the SaaS application or other related services can be utilized.

- Vendor lock-In. Providers may make it very simple to register and acquire a service but difficult to withdraw. For example, it may require internal engineering rework or incur significant cost to transfer SaaS applications from other providers. Not all providers follow standard tools, protocols, and APIs, yet the features offered could be essential for certain business tasks.
- Interoperability. Integration with existing services and

applications can be a huge concern if the SaaS application is not built to comply with available standards for integration. In that event, companies may have to minimize dependencies with SaaS services or build their own integration systems, which is probably not possible all the time.

Popular SaaS solutions

There are so many SaaS solutions available in the market today. Below are some of the well-known ones:

- o **Slack**

  A real-time search, archiving and messaging solution, Slack is readdressing business communication. Users may establish team discussions in open channels assigned to specific projects or topics, or limit more sensitive discussions to private, invite-only members. Colleagues also may converse one-on-one by making use of private, protected direct messages. Slack also allows users to share PDFs, spreadsheets, documents and files, complete with options for highlighting and inserting comments for future reference; moreover, all files, notifications and messages are automatically indexed and archived.

o **Dropbox**

Using Dropbox, users are able to keep documents and files at close reach across all devices. Whatever is inserted into Dropbox storage automatically appears across all mobile and desktop devices, facilitating professionals to start a project on their computer at work, make changes on their smartphone when going home, and add the final edits from their home tablet. Users can also ask coworkers to access a particular Dropbox folder or forward specific images and files accessible via password-protected links; there is an additional remote wipe choice in case of emergency.

- **Google Apps**
  For a while now, Google has expanded beyond its advertising and search roots to offer companies a wide-ranging sets of productivity tools. This comprises of Google Drive,

shared video meetings and calendars, as well as custom professional email (including spam protection). Google Drive is a document storage solution based in the cloud, that allows users to access documents from any system and share them directly with coworkers, in the process removing email attachments along with the hassles of merging several versions.

- **Salesforce.com**
  Perhaps, the ideal SaaS application, Salesforce stays at the frontline of the cloud computing transformation it helped build. The customer relations management product empowers businesses to gather all information on leads,

prospects and customers in a single online platform, permitting authorized employees to access sensitive data on any connected system at any time. Salesforce gives credit to its tools for increasing customer sales to about 37 percent in addition to driving increased customer satisfaction and loyalty.

o **Microsoft Office 365**
Popular Microsoft productivity applications like PowerPoint, Excel and Word are longstanding staples of the workplace; however, Microsoft Office 365 that is based in the cloud dramatically magnifies the Office suite's parameters. With it, users can create, edit and share files from any

Windows, Android, iOS, Mac or PC device in real-time, interact with customers and colleagues across a variety of tools from video conferencing to email and leverage an assortment of collaborative technologies assisting secure interactions both outside and inside of the company.

- ○ **Zendesk**

  This cloud-based support ticketing and customer service platform allows representatives to more efficiently handle inbound client demands across any communications channel — chat, phone, social media, web or email. Features include Zendesk Voice (a cloud-based, integrated phone support solution), Zopim (a real-time chat solution) and Automatic Answers (a tool powered by machine learning for solving and interpreting customer requests and questions). As stated by Zendesk, its business users receive positive ratings for over 86 percent of interactions with their customers.

- **DocuSign**

  This is a transaction management services and electronic signature technology platform that supports the transfer of digital contracts as well as other e-signed files. Users may read, sign and submit business documents from any location, guaranteeing agreements and approvals are executed in minutes, instead of days. DocuSign e-signatures are considered to be legally binding for most personal and business relations in virtually every country across the globe.

- o **Amazon Web Services**
  Amazon has also transformed beyond its main e-commerce platform to assist the on-demand delivery of IT applications and resources based in the cloud, reinforced by pay-as-you-go pricing choices. Currently, Amazon Web Services has more than 70 services, including resources for the Internet of Things, management, deployment, analytics, database, networking, storage, and computing.

- o **Box**
  This virtual workspace allows professionals to work together

with anyone, anywhere.
Customers can securely share
huge files through custom URL
or traditional link, safeguarding
documents and data through
password protection and
permissions. Box supports over
120 file types, and customers
may preview content before
downloading. All content
approval, discussion, editing
and sharing is confined to a
single centralized file, and
customers receive real-time
notifications when changes are
made. Additionally, Box
automates tasks like contract
approvals and employee
onboarding, reducing repetition
and shortening review cycles.

- **Platform-as-a-Service (PaaS)**

  PaaS has to do with cloud computing services that support the development and deployment of web applications. PaaS supports the entire lifecycle of applications, assisting users in building, testing, deploying, managing and updating all in one location — without the complexity and cost of purchasing and management of the underlying software and hardware. The service also includes infrastructure, database management, operating systems, business intelligence solutions, middleware and development tools.

  PaaS delivery

  There is similarity between the delivery model of SaaS and PaaS, except, rather than providing the software through the internet, PaaS delivers a platform for creating software. This platform is delivered through the web, allowing developers to fully concentrate on developing the software without getting concerned about the infrastructure, storage, software updates or operating systems. PaaS allows businesses to create and design applications that are integrated into the PaaS with distinctive software components. These middleware or applications, are highly available and scalable as they adopt certain cloud characteristics.

Characteristics of PaaS

Here are some key features of PaaS model:

- o Facilitates collaborative work even when teams work remotely.

- o Databases and web services are integrated.
- o Several users can retrieve the same development application.
- o It is established on virtualization technology, signifying that resources can simply be scaled down or up according to business changes.
- o Offers an assortment of services to help with developing, testing, and deploying applications.

When to utilize PaaS

PaaS is an appropriate option for modern application Development. If there are several developers engaged in the same development task, or if other providers must also be included, PaaS can offer great flexibility and speed to the whole process. PaaS is also helpful if there is need to create customized applications. It can greatly minimize costs and it can rectify some challenges that arise when speedily developing or deploying an application.

Benefits of PaaS:

- o Efficiently control the application lifecycle. PaaS offers all of the abilities that is needed to support the entire web application lifecycle: development, testing, deployment, management, and maintenance inside the same integrated environment.
- o Support development teams that are in different locations. Since the internet is used to access the development environment, teams can still

collaborate on projects despite the locations of team members.

- Use sophisticated tools inexpensively. A pay-as-you-go system makes it possible for businesses or individuals to use business analytics and intelligence tools and sophisticated development software that they could not manage to purchase outright.

- Develop for several platforms—including mobile—more simply. Some service vendors give development options for several platforms, like browsers, mobile devices, and computers making cross-platform applications easier and faster to develop.

- Add development capacity without adding staff. PaaS features can give development teams new capacity without having to add staff with the required skills.

o Reduce coding time. PaaS development solutions can reduce the time used to develop new applications with pre-coded application features built into the platform, for example search, security features, directory services, workflow, and so on.

o Facilitates easy movement to the hybrid model.

o Automates business policy.

o Minimize complications by using middleware as a service.

Disadvantages of PaaS

The concerns and limitations of PaaS include:

- Operational restriction. Custom-built cloud-based operations administration and automation workflows are probably not applicable to PaaS resources as the platform usually restricts operational capabilities for end-users. Even though this is intended to lessen the operational burden on users, the loss of operational power may influence how PaaS solutions are operated, provisioned and managed.
- Customization of outdated systems: PaaS is probably not a plug-and-play resolution for existing legacy services and applications. Numerous configuration changes and customizations may be necessary for outdated systems

to function with the PaaS solution. The resulting customization may produce a complicated IT system that may restrict the worth of the PaaS investment completely.

o Runtime problems: Other than the restrictions associated with specific services and applications, PaaS deliverables may not be augmented for the frameworks and language needed by a company. Specific framework versions are either not available or do not perform excellently with the PaaS solution, thus development of custom dependencies with the framework will be limited.

o Vendor lock-In. Technical and business requirements that direct decision for a particular

PaaS solution may not be
utilized in the future. If the
provider has not provisioned
appropriate migration policies,
switching to another PaaS
provider may not be likely
without affecting the business.

o   Integrations: There is an
increase in the complexity of
integrating the data stored
inside in-house datacenter or
off-site cloud, and it may affect
which services and applications
can be implemented with the
PaaS offering. Particularly when
not every feature of an outdated
IT system is developed for the
cloud, integrating with existing
infrastructure and services may
be a challenge.

o   Data security: Even though
companies can run their own

services and applications using PaaS resources, the data residing in external cloud servers controlled by providers poses security concerns and risks. The security choices may also be inadequate as users are probably not able to use services with specific hosting procedures.

Popular PaaS solutions

Among the leading PaaS vendors are Heroku, Engine Yard, Mendix, Pivotal, Red Hat, Salesforce.com, IBM, Google, Microsoft, and Amazon Web Services (AWS). Most widely used containers, libraries, languages, and associated tools are available on every major PaaS vendors' clouds. Google, Microsoft, and Amazon in particular offer complete collections of cloud-based solutions including security, management tools, developer tools, mobile backend, networking, analytics, databases, storage, and computing tools. In many situations, these wholly managed services supplement the PaaS solutions in these public clouds. It is no coincidence that many PaaS providers are also leading vendors of software development tools.

Here is a short introduction to some of the popular PaaS offerings:

- o **Pivotal Cloud Foundry**
  This is an open source solution managed through the Cloud Foundry Foundation. Cloud Foundry was initially created by VMware and then moved to Pivotal Software, a collaborative venture by General Electric, VMWare, and EMC. Cloud Foundry is developed for

running and building container-based applications, making use of Kubernetes for orchestration.

o **OpenShift by Red Hat**
OpenShift is a collection of PaaS solutions, which can be deployed on-site or cloud-hosted, for deploying and building containerized applications. The leading resource is the OpenShift Container Platform, which is an on-site PaaS developed around Docker containers that are managed and orchestrated by Kubernetes with Red Hat Enterprise Linux as the foundation.

o **Microsoft Azure Functions**
This can be referred to as a serverless computing framework that allows

developers to operate by connecting to messaging solutions or data sources, making it easy to react and process events. Developers can utilize Azure Functions to develop HTTP-based API endpoints easily reached through a range of applications.

- o **Microsoft Azure App Service**

  This is a completely managed PaaS that integrates BizTalk Services, Mobile Services, and Microsoft Azure Websites into one offering. Azure App Service offers integration between cloud and on-site systems.

- o **Google Cloud Functions**

  This is created to make it simple for developers to scale and run code in the cloud in addition to building event-driven serverless applications.

- **Google App Engine**
This is a PaaS solution for hosting and developing web applications in datacenters managed by Google. Applications are automatically sandboxed, run, and scaled over multiple servers.

- **AWS Lambda**
This serverless, event-driven computing framework runs specified code in response to incidents, and automatically handles the computing resources required by that code. AWS Lambda made the FaaS concept popular, although it predates the term.

- **AWS Elastic Beanstalk**

Using this offering, companies can rapidly manage and deploy applications that are hosted in the AWS Cloud without needing to learn about the framework that controls the applications. This solution automatically handles the specifics of application health monitoring, scaling, load balancing, and capacity provisioning.

- **Infrastructure-as-a-Service (IaaS)**
  IaaS offers on-demand access to computing infrastructure. This includes resources like compute, networks and storage that is required to run workloads. The collection of hardware resources is retrieved from multiple networks and servers usually distributed across several datacenters.

This provides reliability and redundancy to IaaS. A user can request computing services when needed and pay for only what is consumed. IaaS vendors supply a virtual server storage and instance, along with APIs that allow users to transfer workloads to a virtual machine. Users have an assigned storage capacity and can access, configure, stop and start the virtual machine and storage as preferred. IaaS vendors provides small, medium, large, extra-large as well as compute-optimized or memory-optimized instances, along with customized instances, for several workload needs. IaaS delivers the highest level of management control and flexibility over computing resources and is very similar to current IT resources that several IT developers and departments are familiar with today.

IaaS delivery

IaaS delivers cloud computing infrastructure via virtualization technology. These cloud resources are usually provided to the company through an API or a dashboard, and IaaS clients have full control over the whole infrastructure. IaaS offers the same capabilities and technologies as a conventional datacenter without physically maintaining or managing all of it. IaaS customers can still access their storage and servers directly, but this is now outsourced through a cloud-based datacenter.

Different from PaaS or SaaS, IaaS clients have the responsibility of managing features such as data, middleware, operating systems, runtime, and applications. However, IaaS vendors manage the storage, virtualization, networking, hard drives, and servers. Some vendors even provide more services apart from the virtualization layer, for example message queuing or databases.

Characteristics of IaaS

Here are some key features of IaaS model:

- o Flexible and dynamic.
- o Gives full control of the platform to companies.
- o Normally includes several users on one piece of hardware.
- o Services are greatly scalable.
- o The cost differs depending on consumption.
- o Resources are accessible as a service.

- GUI and API-based access.
- Platform virtualization technology.
- Automated administrative tasks.

When to utilize IaaS

IaaS is a great option for a small company or a startup since there's no need to spend money or time trying to create software and hardware. IaaS is also advantageous for large companies that desire to have full control over their infrastructures and applications, but only want to purchase what is actually needed or consumed. For companies that are growing quickly, IaaS can be a worthy option since they do not have to be tied to a specific software or hardware as their requirements evolve and change. IaaS also helps if there is uncertainty about the demands a different application will need, as there is enough flexibility to scale down or up as needed.

Benefits of IaaS

- o Decrease wasted resources. Transparent metering, pricing, and chargeback tools enable IT administrators to identify where costs can be decreased.
- o Quick scalability. Instantly distribute new computing resources to satisfy business demands because of peak periods, company decline or growth.
- o Better agility. Computing resources can be supplied on demand and sent back to the resource pool simply.
- o Greater efficiency. Resources are pooled and virtualized

ensuring physical infrastructure is utilized to maximum capacity.

- o Improved security. With the proper service agreement, vendors can offer security for data and applications that may be superior to what can be attained in-house.
- o Increased supportability, dependability, and stability. With IaaS, it is not required to maintain and upgrade hardware and software or troubleshoot equipment issues. With the right agreement established, the service provider guarantees that a company's infrastructure is dependable and meets service level agreement (SLA).
- o Innovate quickly. As soon as the decision has been made to launch a new initiative or

product, the essential computing infrastructure can be prepared in minutes or hours, instead of the longer length of time it could take to build internally.

o Enhances disaster recovery and business continuity. Attaining high availability, disaster recovery, and business continuity is costly, since it requires a substantial amount of staff and technology. Nevertheless, with the proper SLA established, IaaS can decrease this cost and access data and applications as usual during an outage or disaster.

o Eradicates capital expense and minimizes ongoing cost. IaaS avoids the upfront expense of building and managing an in-house datacenter, making it an efficient choice for start-ups and companies testing new ideas.

Disadvantages of IaaS

The concerns and limitations of IaaS include:

o Multitenant security. Because the hardware resources are automatically distributed across users when requested, the provider is required to guarantee that other clients cannot access data saved in storage assets by previous clients. Likewise, clients must depend on the vendor to make certain that virtual machines are adequately isolated inside the multitenant cloud infrastructure.

- o Internal training and resources. Extra training and resources may be necessary for the employees to learn how to successfully manage the infrastructure. Clients will be responsible for business continuity, backup and data security. However, due to insufficient control of the infrastructure, management and monitoring of the resources may not be easy without adequate resources and training available in-house.

- o Legacy systems working in the cloud. While clients can run legacy applications in the cloud, the framework may not be built to deliver certain controls to protect the legacy applications. Minor improvement to legacy applications may be vital before transferring them to the cloud, it could possibly lead to new security concerns unless the applications are properly tested for performance and security in the IaaS systems.

o Security. Even though the client is in control of the operating systems, middleware, data and applications platform, security issues can still be generated from the host or virtual machines. System vulnerabilities or insider threat may expose data transmission between the virtual machines and host infrastructure to unauthorized entities.

Popular IaaS solutions

- **Digital Ocean**

  This is a cloud computing vendor designed for developers. It offers tools that permits users to control cloud-based servers. Its key features include pre-built open source applications, fast network, highly available storage, simple API, SSD performance, and can deploy in seconds.

- **HP Enterprise Converged System**

  This is a cloud developed on OpenStack, and the IaaS solution is for hybrid, private and public clouds. Its key features include flexible, reduced cost of ownership, and smaller, faster and hyper-converged.

- **IBM SmartCloud**

  This is a cloud solution with high performance, that offers core storage and compute services. This cloud is great for companies that manage higher number of testers and developers.

- **Apache CloudStack**

  This open source cloud computing system was designed to build, deploy and manage IaaS solutions. Its key features include simple template creation process, dynamic workload management, powerful API, secure AJAX console access, brand-able self-service user interface, and rich management user interface.

Chapter 3

Cloud deployment models

Below are the forms of cloud deployment models:

- **Public cloud**

  This form of cloud is typically utilized for Business to Consumer (B2C) related interactions. Cloud service providers manage and own public clouds, while distributing their computing resources, such as commercial infrastructure environments or operating system platform (utilized for testing and software development, storage, servers, applications, virtual machines) through the internet. Services offered could be free or provided via a number of subscription or by-request pricing arrangements, as well as a pay-per-usage format. Users only make payment for the bandwidth, storage or CPU cycles they consume. The public cloud provides a huge array of computing resources and solutions to handle the rising requirements of companies of all verticals and sizes.

How public cloud works

A public cloud has an entirely virtualized infrastructure. Cloud providers develop a multi-tenant infrastructure that allows tenants or users to have common computing resources. However, every user's data remains inaccessible to other users. It also depends on high transmission capacity of network connections for quick data transfer. Storage on public cloud is usually redundant, making use of several datacenters and duplication of file versions. Due to this, it has earned a reputation for flexibility.

A public cloud is possibly the easiest out of the other cloud deployments models: A user demanding more services, platforms or resources, basically pays the provider by the byte or hour to have the right to use needed services on-demand. Cloud-based applications, storage, raw processing power or infrastructure are gotten remotely from hardware maintained by the provider, combined into data groups, coordinated by automation and management software, and transferred through the internet to the user. The users do not possess the tons of storage they utilize; do not administer procedures at the server farm hosting the hardware; and do not regulate the maintenance or security of their cloud-based services, applications, or platforms. Public cloud consumers merely assent to an arrangement, utilize the services offered, and make payment for needed resources.

Public cloud characteristics

The main characteristics of public clouds are:

o The cloud provider administers the virtualization software, provisions the network and preserves the hardware beneath the cloud.

o Distribution of resources could be free or on-demand.

o Tenants within the cloud provider's firewall have common virtual resources and cloud services that are gotten from the cloud provider's group of software, platforms and infrastructure.

- o Facilitates dynamic PaaS for deployment environments and application development in the cloud.
- o Enablement for accessible, flexible IaaS for compute and storage services instantaneously.
- o Provides access to inventive SaaS commercial applications for applications extending from data analytics and transaction administration to customer resource management (CRM).

Public cloud use cases

The public cloud is an appropriate option for the following:

- o Test environments and software development.

- Supplementary resource requests to tackle fluctuating peak demands.
- Services and applications required to carry out business and IT operations.
- Anticipated computing requirements, for example communication solutions for a particular number of users.

Benefits of public cloud

The essential benefits of public clouds include:

- Minimized complexity and requirements on technical proficiency, since the cloud provider has the responsibility of handling the infrastructure.
- The cost savings enables companies to pursue lean growth approaches and

concentrate investments on revolutionary projects.

o Less wasted resources as users only make payment for what they utilize.

o Cost effectiveness. Developing a private cloud can get very costly. There is a need to contemplate the original fee to purchase every hardware required, and then the continuing upkeep, comprising of the manpower or technical experts, the improvement sequence as equipment gets to end-of-life, and hardware failures. A public cloud replaces this with an agreement for a recurrent fee that offers the above without the expensive startup charge. With bigger cloud providers, there are economies of scale, as they host numerous accounts, thus can buy and operate equipment more competently, and at a reduced rate than several companies can achieve independently.

○ Great dependability. The datacenter of most companies is located in a certain geographic site, which may be susceptible to power outages, disastrous weather occurrences, and other probable problems. Only a small percentage of companies have the means to create many datacenters, in many different geographic locations. Nevertheless, when it comes to public cloud, providers like Google and Microsoft are huge operations offering a massive system of servers through countless different parts, offering redundancy, and consequently a greater level of dependability, than most companies can offer independently. If there is an occurrence when one datacenter goes down, the rest would continue operating, and there would be no downtime experienced by the company.

o Scalability. Different from a private cloud, where companies must develop and create the infrastructure, a public cloud denotes the provider is responsible for offering the resources when required. An added advantage to the company is that this enables scaling of resources as desired, and to be alert to the intermittent rise in traffic that happen. For instance, this signifies that companies do not have to overpopulate their private cloud in order to handle an annual increase in demand.

Limitations of public cloud

The downsides to public cloud may include:

o   Movement of data

A recurrent usage for public cloud is storing data remotely, capitalizing on redundancy to evade loss of data. However, issues can crop up when moving data as that will be dependent on internet speeds, plus the possibility of been hindered with congestion problems. In addition, the data can wind up in other countries, where it may be answerable to varying regulations and diverse data privacy laws.

- o Reduced performance
  Private cloud service connection is done through a faster corporate local area network, while public cloud is dependent on the internet connection. This can lead to increase in latency for applications, resulting in lesser performance, specifically since most datacenters can be situated quite far away geographically from their users.
- o Security fears
  Even though public cloud security has enhanced, there are still worries that servers shared with numerous consumers are characteristically not as secure as private cloud services

committed to one company (with the possibility of added security behind the company's firewall). A current case in point of upsetting data leakages are the various 'bucket leaks' through Amazon Web Services from Accenture, GoDaddy, Tesla, and Spyfone.

Public cloud providers

There are tons of public cloud providers in the market, but the more popular ones are Google Cloud, Amazon Web Services, Alibaba Cloud and Microsoft Azure. These vendors offer their services through the internet, or via allocated connections, and utilize a central pay-per-usage method. Every vendor provides a collection of products focused on different enterprise needs and workloads. Some companies view the pay-per-usage method as a smart and more adaptable economic model. For instance, companies justify services acquired through public cloud as variable or operational cost instead of fixed or capital cost. In a few occasions, this indicates that companies do not need advanced budget arrangement or extensive reviews for public cloud choices. Despite that, since consumers usually set up public cloud solutions in a self-service method, a few organizations find it hard to correctly monitor cloud service utilizations, and possibly wind up paying for extra cloud solutions than is needed. Some companies also just have a preference to directly manage and supervise their own internal IT solutions, including servers.

- **Private Cloud**

  This has to do with cloud computing
  solutions utilized entirely by a single
  company. It can be physically situated
  on the organization's internal
  datacenter. A few companies also
  request for the hosting of their private
  cloud by third-party vendors. The
  infrastructure and services in a private
  cloud are retained on a proprietary
  network. Private Cloud can also be
  known as on-premises cloud, internal
  cloud or corporate cloud.

  A private cloud scales back the
  software utilized to operate IaaS public
  clouds into technologies that can be
  installed and run in a user's
  datacenter. Here, in-house clients can
  set up their own cloud resources to
  run, test and build applications, with

measurements to bill departments for resource utilization. The private cloud aids administrators in the process of automating the datacenter, by reducing management and manual provisioning. Examples of private cloud providers include OpenStack and VMware. It is important to note that there is no full conformation of the private cloud to the description of cloud computing. A private cloud requires that a company develop and preserve its own core cloud framework; only the in-house consumers of a private cloud encounter that as a cloud computing solution.

Private cloud permits companies to profit from a few of the benefits of public cloud, without having to worry about surrendering control over services and data, since it is hidden behind the company's firewall. Businesses can control the location for data storage as well as develop their cloud framework as they want (mostly for PaaS or IaaS projects), to offer software developers entry to a collection of resources that scales as needed without jeopardizing security. On the other hand, that supplementary security does not come cheap, as some organizations will have the size and scope of Google, Microsoft or AWS, which suggests that they might not have the capacity to generate similar economies of scale. Regardless, for organizations that demand extra security, private cloud could be an important starting point, aiding in the comprehension of cloud solutions or restructuring in-house applications for deployment in the cloud, before been transferred to the public cloud.

How private cloud works

A private cloud utilizes virtualization to merge hardware resources into shared pools. With this method, there is no need for the cloud to build environments by virtualizing resources individually from a group of different physical infrastructures. An automated process can be configured to collect all required resources from one source. Inserting a layer of management application enables regulatory control over the data, applications, platforms, and infrastructure to be utilized in the cloud by assisting cloud administrators to recover or retain data, oversee integration points, and optimize and track use. By the time the last automation layer is inserted to reduce or replace human involvement with repeatable processes and instructions, the self-service aspect of the cloud is finalized, and that stack of technologies becomes a private cloud.

For a private cloud to function properly, automation, management and virtualization should be able to work well together. This would also depend on the operating system. The flexibility, dependability, and consistency of the operating system directly decides the strength of the connections between the users, automation scripts, virtual data pools, and physical resources. When that operating system is made freely available and developed for companies then the framework holding up the private cloud becomes not only dependable enough to act as a good foundation, but adaptable enough to scale.

Hosted private clouds

When a company sets up a private cloud, it is wholly responsible for every related cost as well as maintaining, managing, and staffing all underlying architecture. However, vendors can also deliver private clouds as part of a hosted private cloud strategy. Hosted private clouds allows clients to retain a private cloud — whether off or on premises—that is managed, configured, and deployed by a third-party provider. It is a cloud distribution option that assists companies with under-skilled or understaffed IT teams deliver improved private cloud infrastructure and services to users.

Private cloud characteristics

The main characteristics of private clouds are:

- Direct management of underlying cloud framework.
- In-house hardware.
- Single tenant framework.
- Resource pooling.
- Broad access. Phones, tablets, laptops, workstations and other devices can access resources stored in the cloud.
- On-demand self-service where users can provision resources without requesting for help from technical staff.
- Delivers sophisticated governance and security intended for a company's explicit requirements.
- Quick flexibility facilitates increasing or reducing capacity

when required and freeing
resources to be utilized by
others when the requirement is
fulfilled.
o Measured service assures that
the users and the company can
measure the amount of
resources utilized, in order for
those resources to be distributed
in a way that optimizes their
uses. These resources could be
user accounts, bandwidth,
processing and storage.

Private cloud use cases
The private cloud is an appropriate
option for the following:
o Companies that have enough
money to invest in high
availability and performance
technologies.

- Government agencies and highly regulated industries.
- Technology businesses that necessitate strong security and management over their technical functions and the underlying framework.
- Large companies that need innovative datacenter technologies to work proficiently and cost-effectively.

Benefits of a private cloud

The essential benefits of private clouds include:

- High SLA efficiency and performance.
- Improved visibility of infrastructural resources.
- Proficient resource provisioning based on needs of the users.

- Secure and dedicated environments that is not accessible by other companies.
- On-demand services by means of policy-based management and self-service user interfaces.
- Increased infrastructural capability to manage large storage and compute demands.
- High efficiency and scalability to meet unforeseeable demands without weakening performance and security.
- Flexibility to modify the framework based on ever-changing technical and business needs of the company. Private clouds can be completely configured by the company using the framework. An in-house cloud architect builds a completely private cloud. This

means that stakeholders can describe the exact architecture required to run internal applications. Hosted private clouds provide similar benefits but does not need on-site installation. Therefore, the company works with a cloud provider to configure and manage a cloud for its private use.

o Compliance to strict regulations as companies can run measures, configurations and protocols to modify security based on distinct workload requests. For companies working in extremely regulated industries, compliance is vital. Private cloud framework offers companies the capability to comply with stringent regulations since sensitive data is stored on hardware that is inaccessible outside the company. This benefit is available via hosted services as well as on-site hardware installations.

o   Private clouds decrease occurrences of underutilized capacity. They enable companies to routinely configure and reconfigure resources as needed, since there is no restriction on the resources by their physical installations. Moreover, depending the company's security practices and policies, private clouds can deliver better security than other cloud models.

o   When there is a requirement for extra computing resources, hybridization expands the solutions of the private cloud to that of public cloud to sustain productivity without having to set up extra physical servers. This will offer cost-effectiveness to companies that require the security provided by a private cloud but also want to take advantage of the benefits of a public cloud service.

Private cloud limitations

A private cloud can present problems if a company does not have predictable computing requirements. When the demand for resources is unstable, a private cloud might not be capable of scaling successfully, costing the company a lot of money in the end.

The downsides to private cloud may include:

- o When comparing the short-term usage of public cloud and private cloud, the private cloud is more expensive with a moderately high overall cost of ownership. Completely private clouds managed in-house require a large initial investment before bringing value to the company. The hardware needed to operate a private cloud is costly and will need a proficient cloud architect to manage, maintain, and set up the environment. Externally managed private clouds, though, can lessen these costs considerably.

- o There might be restricted access to the private cloud for mobile

users due to the high security
procedures in place.

- o The framework may not provide
  great scalability to meet
  unforeseeable requirements if
  the datacenter is restricted to
  in-house computing solutions. It
  may take additional money and
  time to upgrade the private
  cloud's obtainable resources, if
  there is a requirement for extra
  computing resources from the
  private cloud. Normally, this
  process will be lengthier than
  requesting extra resources from
  a public cloud vendor or scaling
  a virtual machine.

- o Private cloud technologies like
  user self-service and increased
  automation can introduce some
  complexity into a company.
  These technologies usually need

an IT team to redesign some of its datacenter frameworks and implement additional management tools. Accordingly, a company might have to reshape or even expand its IT staff to effectively administer a private cloud. This is not the same as the public cloud, where the cloud vendor manages majority of the underlying complexity.

o The company is solely responsible for optimizing capacity utilization in the private cloud model. An underused cloud deployment can cost the company considerably.

Private cloud service providers

Companies that have an interest in adopting private cloud, but have no access to the funds needed to invest in an in-house infrastructure, can profit from utilizing the services of a private cloud service vendor. Some of the popular providers include:

- o Microsoft's Azure Stack conveys the capabilities of an advanced cloud to any company's datacenter. Azure Stack is equipped for hybridization, signifying that companies can completely utilize compliance offerings while profiting from the entire Azure cloud services when necessary.
- o Hewlett Packard Enterprise is one of the strong players in the hybrid and private cloud computing industry for a long

time. They provide strong services with assistance for any business requirement. Users can select the network configurations and hardware required to improve computing and storage needs. Some of their services include Managed Virtual Private Cloud, Helion Managed Private Cloud, Helion CloudSystem hardware, and Helion Cloud Suite software.

o Cisco provides on-request solutions, innovative application performance management and automated container management. Cisco infrastructure offer data security that is in harmony with workloads to improve compliance.

- VMware enables virtualization with its vSphere solution, and for private clouds, Cloud Foundation Software-Defined Data Center (SDDC).
- Dell EMC provides cloud security and management software, as well as private cloud solutions.
- IBM provides cloud orchestration and management tools, cloud security tools, IBM Managed Cloud solutions, together with private cloud hardware.
- Red Hat offers private cloud management deployment through a variety of platforms like Red Hat Cloud Suite for development and management, Gluster Storage, and OpenStack.
- Oracle's Cloud Platform.

- **Hybrid cloud**

  This form of cloud is utilized for either Business-to-Consumer (B2C) or Business-to-Business (B2B). A hybrid cloud utilizes a private cloud core merged with the strategic use and integration of public cloud solutions. Private cloud cannot be truly isolated from the public cloud and the rest of an organization's IT solutions. Several organizations with in-house private clouds will evolve to administer workloads across public clouds, private clouds, and datacenters, thus creating hybrid clouds. By enabling the movement of applications and data and applications between public and private clouds, a hybrid cloud provides a company with more deployment choices, greater flexibility, and assist in improving existing compliance, security, and infrastructure. Companies can implement sensitive applications or mission-critical workloads on the private cloud and utilize the public cloud to manage spikes in demand or workload bursts. The objective of a hybrid cloud is to build a scalable, automated and unified environment that benefit from everything that a public cloud framework can offer, while retaining power over mission-critical data. Some of main reasons for selecting hybrid cloud include the need to avoid additional costs of hardware during expansion of existing datacenter, and for disaster recovery planning.

Hybrid cloud architecture

Constructing a hybrid cloud involves:

o A private cloud that is either built by the company in-house or acquired through a third-party private cloud vendor like OpenStack.

o A public IaaS platform like Google Cloud, Red Hat Certified Cloud, Amazon Web Services, or Microsoft Azure.

o An appropriate wide area network (WAN) or a virtual private network (VPN) connecting both environments. Many of the popular cloud vendors offers users a preconfigured VPN that is bundled together with their subscription packages. If the company decides to utilize preconfigured VPNs, they would need to insulate applications, services and users from vendor-related proprietary technologies and tools or API calls. Putting an agnostic container framework between public cloud resources and services, and users (or the organizational border) increases the capability to transfer from one cloud vendor to a different one during future migrations. Examples of available preconfigured VPNs include OpenStack Public Cloud Passport provided by OpenStack, ExpressRoute offered by Microsoft Azure, Direct Connect offered by Amazon Web Services, and Dedicated Interconnect by Google Cloud.

Hybrid cloud characteristics

The main characteristics of hybrid clouds are:

- o Enables companies to keep sensitive data and critical application inside a private cloud or traditional datacenter infrastructure.
- o Allows companies to capitalize on public cloud resources like IaaS for elastic virtual solutions and SaaS for the newest applications.
- o Expedites portability of services, applications, and data as well as additional options for deployment models.

Use cases for hybrid clouds

The hybrid cloud is an appropriate option for the following:

- Companies serving many verticals that have different performance, regulatory, and IT security requirements. Regulations exist in certain industries in order to safeguard private data. However, not all data may be required to live in a private cloud. Hybrid cloud enables companies to act in accordance with regulations while still taking advantage of expanded computational power. After the European Union introduced the General Data Protection Regulation (GDPR), several companies have distributed their data among many solutions to fulfill the EU regulations while functioning under a separate group of regulations in the United States and other countries. Any company that manages user data globally must conform to these regulations or face severe financial penalties.

- o Improving cloud investments without undermining the value proposition of either private or public cloud models.
- o Enhancing security on current cloud frameworks, like SaaS services that must be distributed through secure private networks.
- o Tactically undertaking cloud investments, in order to continually tradeoff and switch between the best cloud models obtainable in the market.
- o Highly changeable or dynamic workloads. The future is not predictable. A software might

run proficiently in its present environment today but may need extra computing power the next day. A hybrid cloud adjusts to workload requirements, letting service to operate as usual even when workload needs spike. This is known as "cloud bursting," since the workload transfers from one environment into a different environment. For instance, a transactional order entry application that gets substantial demand spikes during holiday period is a possible hybrid cloud candidate. The software could operate in private cloud, but utilize cloud bursting to request for new computing solutions from a public cloud to meet the additional demands.

- o Big data processing. For instance, a company could utilize hybrid cloud storage to keep its stored test, sales, business and other data, and thereafter set up analytical queries to run in the public cloud, by scaling Hadoop or other related analytics systems to assist demanding distributed computing tasks.
- o Companies needing a wider range of computing resources. For instance, a business might utilize the archival or database solutions of a public cloud vendor, but run mission-critical tasks in a private cloud.
- o Introducing a new software with an untested workload brings with it a level of caution. Companies that operate in the

cloud have to deal with some risks whenever they try a new approach. Hybrid cloud diminishes that risk by minimizing the need for a large initial investment. The company can deploy the latest application and only make payment for the resources it utilizes, instead of upfront payment. If the application gets shelved or fails for whatever reason, the company won't have lost a lot of money.

Benefits of hybrid cloud

The essential benefits of hybrid clouds include:

- o Adaptable policy-driven deployment to allocate workloads across private and public framework based on cost, performance and security requirements.

- Public cloud resources are scaled without exposing important business workloads to the basic security threats.
- High dependability as the services are transferred across several datacenters.
- Better security standing as important business workloads run on dedicated frameworks in private clouds while non-sensitive workloads are distributed to public cloud framework to tradeoff for cost investments.
- Better control over data. Fundamentally, the hybrid model offers companies multiple choices so that stakeholders can select a

framework that best suits each distinct use case.

    o Cost savings depending on scale and configuration. Due to the scalability of the hybrid cloud, applications can be deployed, modified and redeployed as needed. That is ideal for peak periods during the course of the year, when it is less expensive to make payment for extra cloud services in the short term than making an investment in a private cloud infrastructure that may not be used in off-peak times.

Hybrid cloud limitations

Although hybrid cloud has some benefits, there are situations where it may not work. The downsides to hybrid cloud may include:

o It can get costly. While costs can be encouraging in some instances, they can become prohibitive in others. It is not cheap to create dedicated private servers. A public cloud model may be more appropriate for smaller companies, especially when weighed against the initial investment costs of creating and maintaining private servers.

o Privacy and security worries. Hybrid clouds raise security by allowing the company select where data and workloads are stored or performed. They also enable the capability for a company's private cloud to stay behind a firewall and then allow scaling up to a public cloud as required, restricting data exposure. On that basis, hybrid clouds can form a bigger attack surface and data passing through cloud networks can be vulnerable to similar security threats as public clouds.

o Hybrid clouds may be a poor choice for software that are latency sensitive. Information transported back and forth between the public and private sections of a hybrid cloud can produce indefensible latency.

o There is complexity involved in building an effective hybrid cloud. Without an appropriate method to connect the two cloud environments, the company is simply managing multiple clouds, and that brings about a less efficient multi-cloud approach, instead of a true hybrid cloud. Private cloud workloads have to gain entrance to and work together with public cloud, therefore, hybrid cloud necessitates solid network connectivity and API compatibility.

o For the public cloud aspect of a hybrid cloud model, there are possible service-level agreements (SLAs) infractions, connectivity issues, and other potential service disruptions. To diminish these risks, companies can design hybrid cloud workloads that can interact with several public cloud vendors. Nonetheless, this can still complicate workload testing and design. In some situations, a company would need to redesign workloads scheduled for hybrid cloud to undertake certain public cloud vendors' APIs.

o Developing and maintaining the private cloud aspect of a hybrid cloud model, would require great expertise from local cloud architects and IT staff. The execution of additional software, like helpdesk systems, databases etc., can further make a private cloud complicated. Besides, the company is entirely responsible for maintaining the private cloud, and must accommodate any modifications to public cloud service and APIs over time.

- **Multicloud**
This is a strategy where a company leverages more than one cloud

computing frameworks to perform several tasks. Companies that want to avoid dependence on a single cloud vendor may decide to utilize resources from several vendors to get the best advantages from each distinct service. A multi-cloud framework may refer to the unification of IaaS, PaaS, and SaaS solution. It may also denote to the utilization of several public and private cloud models. A multi-cloud framework could be all-public, all-private or a mix of both. Companies utilize multi-cloud solutions to allocate computing resources, reduce the risk of data loss and downtime, and increase the available storage and computing power.

Hybrid Cloud vs Multicloud

There's a huge difference between multicloud and hybrid cloud.

Multicloud has to do with the existence of more than one cloud services of the same type (private or public), obtained from different providers. Hybrid cloud involves the existence of multiple deployment models (private or public) with some form of orchestration or integration between them. A multicloud strategy could consist of two private cloud frameworks or two public cloud frameworks. A hybrid cloud strategy could consist of a private cloud framework and a public cloud framework with infrastructure (facilitated by containers, middleware, or application programming interfaces) enabling workload portability. These cloud strategies are mutually exclusive: Both cannot exist at the same time because there is either an interconnection (hybrid cloud), or there's not (multicloud).

Having several cloud models, both private and public, is becoming more standard across companies as they try to improve performance and security through a diversified portfolio of environments.

Importance of containers for multicloud

One of the obstacles of a multicloud strategy is that different cloud services operate in different software frameworks. Companies want to develop software that can simply move across a wide variety of these frameworks without causing integration difficulties. Containers are the best solution because they isolate and package applications from the underlying runtime environment. This enables developers to create software that will run practically anywhere, and also facilitates the company to select public cloud vendors, based on universal standards (for example, cost, space, storage, uptime) rather than on its capability to support the company's workload caused by proprietary limitations. This portability is enabled by microservices, an architectural methodology to creating software where applications are divided into their smallest modules, separate from one another. Microservice-based applications are placed in containers. Most companies are mostly utilizing open source resources to deploy and manage these containerized applications. Kubernetes is an example of a container that has risen as the dominant system for container orchestration.

Reasons to adopt multicloud

A multi-cloud strategy enables organizations to choose different cloud solutions from different vendors because some are more appropriate for specific tasks than others are. For instance, some cloud solutions have incorporated machine-learning capabilities or focus on large data transfers. Companies adopt a multi-cloud strategy for the following reasons:

- o **Vendor lock-in**

    One of the most commonly cited reasons for adopting multicloud is the requirement to prevent becoming locked into a specific cloud provider's pricing model, add-on services, and infrastructure. Cloud-native applications dependent on microservices and containers can certainly be created to be transferrable between clouds, but vendors will usually try to make their frameworks tenacious with certain services and functions that distinguishes them from their competitors. Consequently, a portable application may not utilize a cloud vendor's full potential, leading companies to have to ascertain the trade-off between full functionality and portability -- with possible lock-in -- for specific workloads. The outcome across numerous workloads is possible to be a multicloud strategy.

o **Shadow IT**

A company may wind up with a multicloud approach accidentally, through the agency of shadow IT. Shadow IT is technology utilized by groups or individuals within a company that is not regulated by the company's IT department. This issue tends to come up when the company's requirements are not fully met by policy-compliant IT. Software or hardware deployed separately from the main IT team may get large enough to need more supervision. Thereupon, migrating the data and infrastructure to a preferred model (for example, public cloud) might no longer be possible. That shadow IT deployment becomes integrated into the company's current clouds, thus creating a multicloud.

- **Performance**

  Companies can reduce latency as well as other performance metrics, like packet loss and jitter, by selecting a cloud vendor with datacenters that are physically close to their clients, since performance is usually inversely associated with the amount of network hops amongst servers. For companies that have a broad range of workloads in the cloud, the ideal solution is probably to use multiple cloud providers.

- **Compliance**

  Several multicloud infrastructures can help companies achieve their goals for compliance regulations, risk management, and governance. Data governance requirements -

- for example, the EU's GDPR --
will sometimes make sure that
customer data is stored in
specified locations. Unless
companies intend to build and
maintain their own on-site data
lakes, a multicloud approach
might be required, depending
on a company's workload mix
and geographical distribution.

o **Resilience**
Every cloud provider –
including large ones with
several geographically
distributed, redundant
datacenters -- undergo outages
intermittently, so using only one
provider may lead to the
unavailability of mission-critical
application. A multicloud
approach may bring
management and deployment

concerns, but it may also bring about better resilience, disaster recovery, failover, and security. Cloud solutions like Google Cloud Platform, Microsoft Azure, and AWS deliver information on outages, but the differences in reporting make comparisons tricky. It is necessary to carry out proper research to comprehend the historical and geographical performance of the cloud solution been considered.

Multicloud automation and management

Information Technology is getting more dynamic due to virtual infrastructure both on-site and off-site. This presents significant complexity around capacity planning, financial controls, resource management, compliance and governance, and self-service. Cloud automation and management tools assists in maintaining greater oversight and visibility across these different resources. Automation has been utilized discretely within companies, with disparate tools utilized by different teams for different management domains. Nevertheless, existing automation technologies have the capability to automate assets across environments. Inserting modern automation proficiency to multicloud environments restricts the environment's complexity while improving workload performance and security for cloud-native and traditional applications.

Benefits of multicloud strategy

A multi-cloud offers options to a company. With more choices comes the capacity to capitalize on digital modification without getting locked into one service or raising a substantial initial capital. The essential benefits of multicloud include:

- o **Enhanced disaster preparedness**

  The possibility of concurrent downtime across several cloud providers is extremely low. Cloud service vendors like Amazon Web Services, Microsoft Azure, and Google Cloud Platform have remarkable service level agreements that safeguards their customers against downtime. By making use of more than two of these solutions, risk of disaster declines significantly.

- o **Dependable architecture**
  Making use of more than one cloud services creates redundancies that minimizes the risk of a single point of failure. Multicloud diminishes the possibility that downtime in one service will take the whole company offline. Adding hybridization inserts an additional level of security by storing sensitive data inside a secure, local network.

- o **Freedom of choice**
  A single cloud vendor may not be capable of providing a company with every computing services it requires. Several financial stakeholders may also be cautious of provider lock-in.

If the company finds a better offer with a different provider, it may become challenging to pull away from an infrastructure that is originally designed for a different provider's cloud environment.

- o **Improved security**
  Just like hybrid cloud, multicloud empowers companies by maintaining strong security compliance while enhancing computing resources. It also minimizes the risk of downtime in mission-critical applications due to a dispersed denial of service (DDoS) attack. When even one hour of interruption can cost a company a lot financially, advanced security practices pay for themselves.

- **Optimized return on investment**

  A multi-cloud approach enables stakeholders to select the specific services that operate best for their company. As different business requirements arise, modify and become more complicated, the company can allocate resources for particular uses, take full advantage of those resources and only pay for what is actually used.

- **Lower latency**

  Organizations should choose cloud zones and regions that are geographically closer to their customers to reduce latency and enhance user experience. The lesser the distance for data to travel, the quicker the application will respond. All providers have cloud regions all over the world, but a single vendor may have a datacenter nearer to the customers. Utilizing a combination of several cloud providers to achieve quicker speed may be beneficial to improve applications' user experience.

- ○ **Negotiating strength**
  Competition holds a lot of power. A bigger company with high spend and usage may have a higher negotiating power if more than two cloud providers are pitted against each other for its business. They can leverage the diverse pricing options between providers to select the service that gives them the best value.

- **Innovation**

  Multicloud strategy gives the flexibility to innovate quickly while getting the most out of the best-in-class or unique groups of services every cloud vendor offers. This allows developers to concentrate on innovation without compromising to meet the restrictions of one cloud vendor over another. Different from the legacy organizational method where the provider dictated the infrastructure of the enterprise applications via the features. While all cloud vendors compete to provide the best toolsets and services for everything an organization need to achieve, a multicloud strategy allows the company to choose the services and provider that best fit their needs. For example, AWS may be the best solution for video encoding, but Google Cloud may be the only cloud for annotation videos and making them searchable. Each cloud vendor has its weaknesses and strengths. Depending on the components needed to incorporate into an application, a company can select the best solutions from each vendor to build the application.

Disadvantages of multicloud

Developing and running a multicloud infrastructure comes with a distinct set of challenges. Some of the key concerns to examine before implementing a multicloud strategy are:

- **Operational overhead**

  Multi-cloud can get complicated as far as operational management is concerned. With a company's infrastructure spread out over several clouds, consideration of regular administrative tasks – like how to access resources, backup data, consolidate logs, notify and respond to events, monitor applications and services, and patch operating systems – add extra layers of complexity. All cloud vendors have integrated solutions for every one of these operational domains. A company can decide to utilize these value-add solutions that can be tightly incorporated with one another to maximize value from each vendor's service or they can try to abstract all or some of these to gain effectiveness. Regardless, there are trade-offs between value, timeliness, and convenience.

- ○ **Security risks**

  During operations with a single cloud vendor, a company can leverage their expertise and tools to handle the security of their applications' data, access compliance requirements and permissions. Applications become more complicated and have a broader attack surface when running on numerous clouds, which raises the probability of a security breach. Constructing a secure network with incident response, virus protection, WAF, firewalls, and IDS/IPS for one cloud is not a simple process. Companies must determine how they will respond to, log, alert, manage, and configure security events across numerous clouds. In addition, consideration of how to control resource policies, secrets management, SSL/TLS encryption, access and identity management, and encryption key, across several cloud providers. Utilizing third-party solutions may help reduce some security risk, but the security of a multicloud infrastructure can be considerably more difficult than with one cloud provider.

o **Cost reporting, optimization and estimation**

Although companies can save costs by utilizing multiple cloud providers, consolidating cost estimation, chargeback, and costs gets more difficult. Each cloud vendor has different costs for each solution offered and to correctly estimate costs, the company will need appropriate knowledge of the pricing structure of all the services been used. In terms of billing and usage, there is a necessity to have cross-account cost optimization and reporting tools set up to efficiently handle the financial aspects of utilizing services across several clouds. In some circumstances, the movement of data between clouds can lead to an increase in costs because of the elevated costs of moving data from one cloud and into a different cloud provider.

- o **Talent management**
  There is a high demand for cloud professionals. It's not easy to recruit for cloud architects and engineers with knowledge and experience of a single cloud vendor. Finding security experts, engineers, and developers with knowledge of several clouds is very difficult. A company will have to discover the right people to work on several cloud platforms, secure several infrastructures, and operate and manage across several clouds.
- o **Different APIs**
  Different providers offer services with varying application setup, requiring

different forms of managing the APIs. This can be achieved with specialized tools to accomplish seamless management and deployment even with combinations of various services.

Chapter 4

Virtualization and Cloud Computing

Virtualization is the main facilitating technology for Cloud Computing. Virtualization is technology that enables users to create numerous dedicated resources or simulated environments from a single, physical system. Software known as a hypervisor links straight to that hardware and enables users to split one system into separate, unique, and secure environments called virtual machines. These virtual machines depend on the hypervisor's capability to separate the system's resources out of the hardware and allocate them appropriately.

With the assistance of Virtualization, multiple applications and operating systems can run on similar Machine and its equivalent hardware simultaneously, increasing the flexibility and use of hardware.

To put it simply, one of the key cost saving, hardware reducing, energy efficient strategy used by cloud vendors is virtualization. Virtualization allows sharing of a single physical representation of an application or a resource among multiple businesses and customers on one occasion. It does this by giving a rational name to a physical resource and offering a pointer to that resource on-demand. The word virtualization is often identical with hardware virtualization, which portrays a fundamental role in competently delivering Infrastructure-as-a-Service (IaaS) resources for cloud computing. Besides, virtualization technologies deliver a virtual framework for not only implementing applications but also for networking, memory, and storage.

Benefits of virtualization
- Increases cost savings with decreased hardware expenditure.

- Provides for easier disaster recovery and backup.
- Provides capability to manage resources effectively.
- Decreased risk of data loss, since data is backed up on several storage locations.
- Increased employee productivity due to better accessibility.
- Removal of special utility and hardware requirements.
- Smaller footprint due to lower workforce, energy and hardware requirements.
- Maximization of server capabilities, thus reducing operation and maintenance costs.
- Enables running several operating systems.

Downsides of virtualization

- Necessity to train IT employees in virtualization.
- Software licensing costs.

Types of virtualization

Virtualization can take various forms based on the type of hardware utilization and application use. Below are the main types:

- **Server/hardware virtualization**
  This operates on the notion that an individual independent piece of a physical server or hardware, may be composed of multiple smaller hardware pieces or servers, basically consolidating many physical servers into logical servers that operate on a single principal physical server. Each little server can host a logical machine, but the whole cluster of servers is regarded as one device by all processes requesting the hardware. The

hypervisor distributes the hardware resource. The main advantages include improved processing power due to application uptime and maximized hardware utilization.

Server/Hardware virtualization is further sectioned into the subsequent types:

- o Paravirtualization – there is no simulation of the hardware, and the guest software operate their own isolated domains.
- o Emulation virtualization – Here, unmodified software operates in modified operating system as a separate system.
- o Full virtualization – Here, the entire simulation of the physical hardware occurs, to allow software to operate an

unmodified guest operating system.

- **Software virtualization**

  It offers the ability to the core computer to run and build one or more virtual frameworks. It produces a computer system equipped with hardware that allows the guest OS to run.

  Software virtualization is further sectioned into the subsequent types:

  - Service virtualization – hosts specific services and processes associated to a particular application.
  - Application virtualization – hosts separate applications in a virtual framework different from the native operating system.

- Operating system virtualization
  – hosts several operating
  systems on the native operating
  system.

- **Memory virtualization**

  It presents a way to disconnect
  memory from the server in order to
  provide a networked, distributed or
  shared function. It improves
  performance by offering greater
  memory size without any modification
  to the core memory. That is why a part
  of the disk drive functions as an
  extension of core computing memory.
  Memory virtualization is further
  sectioned into the subsequent types:
  - Operating system level
    consolidation – An operating
    system provides access to the
    memory pool.

o Application-level consolidation
– Applications operating on
connected computers directly
access the memory pool via the
file system or an API.

- **Storage virtualization**
  Several network storage resources are
  introduced as one storage device to
  make it easier and more efficient to
  manage these resources. This provides
  numerous advantages like automated
  management, improved storage use,
  reduced downtime, easy updates and
  better availability, and enhanced
  storage management in a diverse IT
  environment.
  Storage virtualization is further
  sectioned into the subsequent types:
  o File virtualization - Storage
  system allows entry to files that

are deposited over multiple
hosts.

o Block virtualization - Numerous
storage devices are merged into
one.

- **Network virtualization**
It refers to the monitoring and
management of a network as one
managerial entity from one software-
based administrator's console. The
purpose is to facilitate network
optimization of security, flexibility,
reliability, scalability, and data
transfer rates. It also automates
various network administrative
functions. Network virtualization is
especially useful for networks that
encounter a huge, fast, and irregular
traffic increase. The intended outcome
of network virtualization provides

better network efficiency and productivity.

Network virtualization is further sectioned into the subsequent categories:

- o External: Combine numerous networks, or segments of networks into a simulated unit.
- o Internal: Provide network like capabilities to a single system.

- **Desktop virtualization**

  This is possibly the most common type of virtualization for any proper IT staff. The user's desktop is saved on a remote server, letting the user access the virtual desktop from any location or device. Staffs can conveniently work from home.

- **Data virtualization**

  It allows easily manipulation of data.
  The data is introduced as an abstract
  layer fully independent of database
  systems and data structure. This
  reduces data formatting and input
  errors.

Chapter 5

Cloud Computing vs Grid Computing

Grid computing is an infrastructure that connects computing resources like storage, workstations, servers and PCs and delivers the mechanism needed to access them. It is a middleware to manage different IT resources over a network, enabling them to operate as one. It is mostly utilized in universities for educational reasons and in scientific research. Grid computing and cloud computing is often mixed up, although their operations are almost alike, their operational strategies are different. Table below explains this more clearly.

Cloud Computing	Grid Computing
Cloud-based applications are business specific applications like web-based	Focus on research-based application with the aid of distributed independent

Cloud Computing	Grid Computing
application for handheld devices or thin clients	administrative components working together to resolve a larger computing issue
Client-server architecture	Distributed computing architecture
Centralized management	Decentralized management system where diverse sites are spread around the world, and every site has independent administrations
Pay-as-you-go model	No defined business model
Cloud services are scalable, real-time and highly flexible	Scheduled services with minimal flexibility

Cloud Computing	Grid Computing
Cloud doesn't have provision for interoperability and can cause vendor lock-in	Easily deals with interoperability
Resources can be utilized in a centralized or very rarely in a decentralized way	Resources are utilized in a decentralized way
Huge pool of resources	Limited resources

Chapter 6

Cloud Computing Adoption

While migrating to the cloud is a good step, it is important to proceed with caution. Irrespective of whether the company is looking at a single workload, numerous workloads, or a whole portfolio, converting from on-site to cloud-based IT necessitates more than just comprehending the technology. Effective cloud adoption requires accurate focus and a thorough blueprint, as a single mistake can become time consuming and expensive. Following a formal strategy to executing a cloud solution, reduces risk, accelerates time-to-value, and streamlines the transformation.

- **Learn from other companies**
  Nowadays, there is an increasing number of companies migrating to the cloud. Even though each company's requirements may vary, there is still

some useful lessons to learn from them. Carry out extensive research of other companies with similar capacity and size, to find out what they did to improve their IT department, their process of cloud adoption, mistakes made, and lessons learned.

- **Evaluate the cloud services and providers**

  IT decision makers and executives must assess the challenges and opportunities of adopting a cloud computing approach in their marketplace. Once companies have concluded their research, they must develop their specific cloud approach. IT leaders should choose services and platforms that are quick to market and widely known to their industry. Decision should also be made between multicloud, hybrid, private or public cloud. When assessing provider options, focus should not be only on pricing, take other factors like continuous support, scalability and reliability into account.

- **Legacy application remediation** Current applications will have to be restructured at the application and infrastructure layers to adapt to the capacity and security requirements of the cloud. These applications should be integrated with security and operate in a more automated manner. This requires significant consideration from application teams. Companies can address this challenge by creating a distinct business case for modernization of legacy applications, aligning the migration plan with major application replacements or upgrades, and implementing foundational solutions (like API frameworks) for easier remediation.

- **Cultivate the appropriate skills**
  Professionals should be able to build cloud-based applications rapidly and securely. To accomplish this, organizations will need to employ and train cloud specialists, upskill or retrain the current employees, and establish digital-innovation labs as required with focus on cloud development.

- **Security**
  Companies should take care to confirm that application programming interfaces and software user interfaces are secure and updated. Consistent monitoring and management of reputable tools will assist in protecting against unforeseen and malicious errors and breaches. Program bugs enables hackers to steal data or take control of cloud infrastructures. Monitoring system updates and

quickly detecting vulnerabilities can help remove this risk. Inadequate due diligence in implementing cloud technologies, accidental deletion, and natural disasters can lead to malicious attacks and data loss. Companies of all sizes must create employee training programs and a cloud computing roadmap to mitigate these issues.

Chapter 7

Conclusion

Cloud computing has to do with providing computing power (software, operating system, storage, network, RAM, CPU) as a service over the internet instead of physically having the computing solutions at the customer location. There are three types of cloud computing, commonly referred to as Software-as-a-Service (SaaS), Platform-as-a-Service (PaaS), and Infrastructure-as-a-Service (IaaS). Cloud deployment models include multicloud, hybrid cloud, private cloud and public cloud. Virtualization is the main facilitating technology for Cloud Computing. Virtualization is technology that enables users to create numerous dedicated resources or simulated environments from a single, physical system. Grid computing and cloud computing is often mixed up, although their operations are almost alike, their operational strategies are different. When adopting cloud computing, there are some steps to consider which include security strategy, cultivating the appropriate skills, legacy application remediation, evaluating cloud services and providers, as well as learning from other companies.

Other Books by Same Author
Productive DevOps: Your Complete

Handbook on Building a Dependable, Agile

and Secure Organization

www.ingramcontent.com/pod-product-compliance
Lightning Source LLC
Chambersburg PA
CBHW031221050326
40689CB00009B/1421

* 9 7 8 1 0 8 6 0 3 9 5 0 4 *